ANIMALS IN THE WILD

AFRICAN WILDLIFE

BABY ANIMALS

BEARS

BIG CATS

DEER, ELK & MOUNTAIN GOATS

ELEPHANTS

GORILLAS

LIONS

MONKEYS & APES

PANDAS

TIGERS

WOLVES

DEER, ELK & MOUNTAIN GOATS

PAUL STERRY

ABOUT THE AUTHOR

PAUL STERRY is the author of numerous books on the subjects of wildlife and natural history. He holds a Ph.D. in zoology from the University of London and has been a research fellow at Sussex University. A world traveler, Mr. Sterry has photographed and studied natural history subjects in places as diverse as the Amazon, the Galapagos, and Alaska. He lives in Hampshire, England.

MASON CREST

MASON CREST
450 Parkway Drive, Suite D
Broomall, Pennsylvania 19008
(866) MCP-BOOK (toll-free)

First printing
9 8 7 6 5 4 3 2 1

ISBN (hardback) 978-1-4222-4168-4
ISBN (series) 978-1-4222-4163-9
ISBN (ebook) 978-1-4222-7635-8

Cataloging-in-Publication Data on file with the Library of Congress

QR CODES AND LINKS TO THIRD-PARTY CONTENT
You may gain access to certain third-party content ("Third-Party Sites") by scanning and using the QR Codes that appear in this publication (the "QR Codes"). We do not operate or control in any respect any information, products, or services on such Third-Party Sites linked to by us via the QR Codes included in this publication, and we assume no responsibility for any materials you may access using the QR Codes. Your use of the QR Codes may be subject to terms, limitations or restrictions set forth in the applicable terms of use or otherwise established by the owners of the Third-Party Sites. Our linking to such Third-Party Sites via the QR Codes does not imply an endorsement or sponsorship of such Third-Party Sites, or the information, products, or services offered on or through the Third- Party Sites, nor does it imply an endorsement or sponsorship of this publication by the owners of such Third-Party Sites.

PHOTO CREDITS

INTRODUCTION

Although outwardly these impala may appear calm and relaxed, they are ever alert for danger. This elegant antelope's sensitive ears and nose are its first line of defense against the stealthy approach of lions, leopards, or hyenas.

Deer, antelopes, goats, sheep, and their relatives are among the most familiar of all mammals. As a group, they are mostly large and relatively easy to see, and many species are closely linked with the spread of humans and the advancement of civilization. Our early ancestors hunted antelopes on the plains of Africa and then turned their attention to species of deer, goats, and sheep as human populations swept across Asia and Europe.

Representatives of the group often favor wild and remote habitats and, for many people, conjure up images of untamed spirits roaming free. So it is perhaps slightly ironic that a handful of the group's members—cattle, sheep, and goats—should have proven so suited to domestication. Their influence on the development, history, and demography of human civilization is inestimable, and they continue to have a profound bearing on society today. Indeed, the manner and densities in which they are farmed often have a huge impact on the habitats in which they are kept; except in a few cases, the effect on the environment generally is a negative one.

The majority of the animals included in this book have in common the appearance of bony outgrowths from their skulls. These can take the form of antlers—seen in most male deer—which are shed and regrown each year, or of horns—seen in most sheep, goats, and antelopes—which are retained throughout life. Antlers and horns perform a variety of functions.

Eyeing each other with apparent disdain, these two Dall's sheep rams need little provocation to begin bouts of head butting to establish or maintain the male hierarchy.

They serve as defensive weapons for many species and in a few cases actually assist in feeding. For the most part, however, their main, if not sole, function is one of display, a male's fitness often being judged by the size of his antlers or horns. Some species dispense with the niceties of ritualized display, and the males do bloody battle with one another. Skull outgrowths may be present or absent and can be formed in different ways, but

there is one factor that unites all the animals in this book: their classification as ruminants, animals with a very special means of digesting their herbivorous diet.

During September and October, other concerns are forgotten as red deer stags devote all their energies to the annual rut. Their roaring calls, sometimes called "belling," carry over considerable distances on calm, misty mornings.

VARIED CREATURES

All the animals considered here belong to a large and important group of herbivorous mammals called the ungulates: animals whose feet bear hooves rather than claws. Horses, rhinoceroses, and their relatives make up one subdivision of this group, while the remainder are known as even-toed ungulates, a varied group that includes familiar species such as pigs, hippos, and camels. What sets apart the deer, antelopes, cattle, sheep, and goats from these other animals is an adaptation in the digestive system. Like all herbivores, their bodies must break down plant cells, and they do so by using a modified gut, a fermentation mode of digestion, and a chewing method known as *rumination*.

The scientific classification of animals places all ruminant mammals in a subdivision of the even-toed ungulates called the Ruminantia. Within this group there are five family divisions: mouse deer, musk deer, true deer, giraffes, and bovids. The last family is a large and complex one whose members include cattle, antelopes, goats, and sheep.

Mouse Deer

Scientists consider mouse deer to be the most primitive of the ruminants. As their name suggests, they are also among the smallest; full-grown adults of most species stand little more than 12 inches (4.75 centimeters) high at the shoulder. The family has representatives in equatorial Africa—the water chevrotain—and south Asia—the mouse deer—and comprises four species.

Mouse deer are essentially solitary animals for much of their lives. They are extremely difficult to observe because of their small size and retiring nature as well as their nocturnal habits and coats marked with cryptic spots and stripes. Mouse deer communicate with one another by sound and smell; urine and feces and the animal's scent mark of musk-like secretions help demarcate territories.

The digestive systems of mouse deer indicate their kinship to other ruminants, although they lack the antlers or horns that characterize so many other members of the group. The rather bizarre facial appearance of mouse deer is further enhanced by the needle-like upper canines projecting downward from the mouth. These teeth grow throughout life and are longer in males than females. The presence of four, fully developed toes also sets mouse deer apart from other ruminants.

Following page: Impala are one of the most widespread and familiar of all Africa's antelopes. They are generally encountered in small herds and favor open savannah woodland rather than the grassy plains exploited by many of their cousins.

A fine set of antlers and a loud, bellowing roar are an elk stag's main attributes during the rutting season. This seasonal exercise is so exhausting for the males that many succumb if the winter that follows is a severe one.

Alerted by the scent of a predator, these white-tailed deer panic and take off at great speed. In a state of alarm, the deer demonstrate the origin of their name. The sight of a white "flag" is a sign to other whitetails that danger threatens.

7

Against a backdrop of stunning fall colors, this bull moose is establishing his place in the annual rut. Compared to some of his rivals, this individual's antlers are rather small, and his chances of assuming a dominant position in the hierarchy in this particular year are slight.

Musk Deer

Despite the striking similarities between musk deer and true deer, these intriguing animals, three species in all, are classified separately. They lack the antlers seen in the males of true deer and have instead extremely long, protruding upper canines, which they use in disputes during rutting season and in defense against predators.

Musk deer live in the hill and upland forests of eastern Asia and are generally solitary except during the breeding season. As their name suggests, the species produces musk, which is used in the perfume trade. This strong-smelling secretion is produced from a musk bag on the underside of the male animals and is used to mark territories.

Deer

Although deer vary in size from the tiny dog-sized muntjac to the huge and impressive moose, all the 36 species have characteristics in common that make their family kinship instantly recognizable. In comparison with many other ruminants, they are rather elegant animals with well-proportioned necks and bodies and proportionately long legs. The head is usually rather triangular in profile, with large ears and eyes. Most noticeable of course are the antlers that project from the heads of most male deer for at least part of the year.

Moose are the largest deer in the world. They stand some 6.5 feet (2 meters) at the shoulder and weigh 1,100 to 1,300 pounds (500 to 600 kilograms) for females and 1,300 to 1,800 pounds (600 to 800 kilograms) for males. Although they are widespread across the northern latitudes in North America, Siberia, and northern Europe, they are probably easiest to see in the New World. Confusingly, when this animal occurs in Europe, it is known as an elk. However, Europeans refer to the same animal in its North American habitat as the moose.

In appearance moose are quite different from other deer, having extremely long legs, an elongated and strangely rounded muzzle, and a long dewlap of skin hanging from the throat. As might be expected in an animal of this size, the antlers are also of gigantic proportions—broad and flattened with fingerlike projections splayed around the margins.

Red deer have widespread but patchy distribution across Europe, the result of their preference for open, untamed habitat combined with the pressures of local extermination by hunting. In common with most other northern temperate deer species, the young are born in the spring, and the cycle begins again at an annual autumn rut at which males compete for the right to mate with females. The species is perhaps easiest to see in Scotland where genuinely wild herds roam the moors and glens. In the absence of any significant wild predators—wolves and bears are long extinct in Great Britain—red deer numbers are thought to pose problems for the regeneration of native pine forests, and there is a strong case for controlling their numbers by shooting. Unfortunately, as with other hunted species, it is often the mature males with the best sets of antlers that are shot, an approach opposite to the process of natural selection where survival of the fittest and strongest is the rule.

In many respects, wapiti, most commonly known in Canada and the United States as elk, are the North American counterparts of Europe's red deer. The species is perhaps more plentiful in and around the Rocky Mountains and also has a foothold in northeast Asia. It is essentially a herd animal, mixed-sex herds being found throughout the winter months. In summer, prior to the autumn rut, mature males split from the females and youngsters in preparation for the rigors to come. Due to the species' popularity among hunters and the high proportion of mature males with good trophy antlers that are taken, the social structure and male hierarchy of many populations are continually and severely disrupted. Wapiti are partial migrants, feeding in pastures on mountain slopes during spring and summer and moving to lower elevations for the winter.

North America is home to two other common deer species, the white-tailed deer and the mule deer—or black-tailed deer. Both are essentially animals of forest, woodland, and scrub, but will

Having thwarted his rivals' claims to his herd, this red deer stag can now mate with the females in turn, as each one comes into season. He must still be vigilant, however, because in unguarded moments interloping males quickly appear on the scene.

Mule deer—sometimes known as black-tailed deer—are hardy animals, used to the rigors of the North American winter. In places where they are not persecuted, this species becomes almost indifferent to the presence of people and can be watched at close quarters.

visit farmland to feed if the opportunity arises. Farther north in North America, caribou are widespread in arctic and subarctic regions.

The precise natural distribution of some deer has been complicated by people's introduction of certain species to far-flung parts of the world. Thus red deer, essentially European animals, occur in New Zealand, while muntjacs, originally from Asia, are now widespread in southern England. The deer family does, however, have indigenous representatives on all continents except Australia and Antarctica, although in Africa, they have only a tiny foothold in the north—this continent is largely the domain of antelopes and gazelles.

The herbivorous diet of deer is satisfied in one of two general ways. Some species feed by grazing on grasses and other low-growing plants, while others browse on leaves and

Almost overnight, the Alaskan tundra assumes the dramatic colors of autumn. This seasonal change corresponds with a switch in the behavior of the region's caribou: The annual rut begins, and within a few weeks, the herds begin migrating south.

shoots at head height. There is, of course, considerable overlap between the two methods of feeding. By and large, deer that graze tend to be herd animals, favoring open, grassy feeding areas close to the cover of woodland or scrub. Browsing deer are more likely to be solitary animals that prefer more wooded terrain than their grazing cousins.

Giraffes

The giraffe needs little introduction. These immensely tall, long-legged, long-necked ruminants occur widely throughout sub-Saharan Africa, their precise distribution determined by the occurrence of the open, savannah woodland they like. As expected with such a tall animal, giraffes are almost exclusively browsers.

Opinions differ regarding the classification of giraffes. Some authorities maintain there is a single species represented by as many as nine subspecies, while others assert that some of these subspecies, for example, the reticulated giraffe, are species in their own right. However, the giraffe family includes one species that is clearly distinct and separate: the intriguing okapi, a forest-dwelling species restricted to a few areas of Zaire.

Bovids

The bovid family is divided into six subfamilies: pronghorn, wild cattle, duikers, grazing antelopes, gazelles and relatives, and goat antelopes, which include sheep and goats.

Pronghorn

The pronghorn is the sole representative of the group, and its range is restricted to the remaining prairie lands of the American Midwest. Along with its open-country companion, the North American bison, pronghorns were driven close to extinction from a population that could be numbered in the tens of millions.

The reticulated giraffe, along with others of its kind, is a browsing animal whose height allows it to exploit foliage unavailable to other potential competitors. This particular giraffe—there are several strikingly different races—is found in the arid country of northern Kenya.

Fortunately, its survival has been ensured by active conservation measures, and today relatively good numbers can be found in protected or controlled areas.

Pronghorns are primarily grazing animals that feed on a succession of grasses, herbaceous plants, and shrubs according to the season. The animals live in herds for much of the year, although males become territorial during the breeding season. Large eyes and a wide range of vision allow pronghorns to spot danger at a distance, and with the capability of running up to 50 miles (30 kilometers) per hour, they can escape from almost any predator.

Wild Cattle and Their Relatives

Members of this subfamily include some of the most familiar wild ruminants. The domesticated descendants of some of the group's members, notably cattle and water buffalo, are among the most important of all animals to man. Wild representatives of the subfamily Bovinae can be found in North America, Africa, and southern Asia. As well as typical cattle-like species, a number of antelope-like ruminants are also placed in the subfamily.

Winter is a time of hardship for many North American animals including the pronghorn. Somehow, however, this extraordinary animal manages to find enough to eat on the prairie grasslands, even when they are covered by a blanket of snow. The horns are occasionally used to expose the vegetation if conditions are severe.

Arguably, the best-known member of the group is the bison. The saga of its wholesale slaughter in the 19th century is one of the sorriest tales associated with the colonization of the continent and one that is inextricably linked to the loss of lands suffered by Native Americans. At one point the species was close to extinction, but fortunately sizable herds have been formed from the small, scattered populations that survived. Sadly, the large herds, numbering countless millions of animals, will never be seen again. This is due to the fact that the vast prairies that once stretched for thousands of miles have now disappeared under cultivation and are unlikely ever to return to their natural state. Bison reserves and national parks offer the only opportunities to see this most American of animals.

Other examples of typical wild cattle and their relatives include the European bison—once extinct in the wild but now established as wild populations in Poland—and the African buffalo, which is one of the most widespread and easily seen game animals on the continent. In Asia, the latter species has a counterpart in the wild water buffalo, although the domesticated animals vastly outnumber their ancestors. The region also boasts gaur, sometimes known as Asian bison, and that most hardy of creatures, the yak, which lives in the Himalayas both in the wild and in domestication. More atypical members of the wild cattle family include the nilgai and four-horned antelope from India and nine species of so-called spiral-horned antelopes from Africa; these include the eland, the sitatunga, the bushbuck, the lesser kudu, and the greater kudu.

Duikers

These charming and fascinating ruminants are found only in sub-Saharan Africa, where they live unobtrusive and rather secretive lives, much of their activity taking place at night. All but one of the seventeen duiker species are forest animals, which adds greatly to the difficulty of observing these creatures. The exception is the common duiker, which favors savannahs, woodlands, and grasslands.

Immense herds of North American bison once roamed the continent's plains, but sadly, this magnificent animal is now restricted to special sanctuaries and national parks in both the United States and Canada. On a positive note, the species is no longer in any danger of extinction within these refuges.

Although many of southern Africa's mammals are adapted to cope with arid conditions for much of the year, most species, including this greater kudu, pay regular visits to permanent water holes. They must remain vigilant, however, because they are especially vulnerable to predators while drinking.

As a group, duikers are all remarkably similar in terms of size and basic body plan. They range in length from about 2 to 3 feet (60 to 90 centimeters), depending on the species, and have relatively compact bodies, short tails, and rather short legs—the back pair being longer than the front pair. The head always appears relatively large for the size of the body, and in most species, both sexes have short, backward-pointing horns. On occasion, duikers are known to supplement their herbivorous diet with small animals.

Grazing Antelopes

Grazing antelopes can be found throughout most of Africa except in the north. The barrier of the Sahara Desert has prevented their spread to this region, though a single species is found over in the Arabian Peninsula. The subfamily consists of 24 species, with representatives adapted to exploit every African habitat where grasses and other low-growing plants are found. Thus, grazing antelopes occur in sites as diverse as swamps and wetlands, arid semideserts, montane grasslands, and open savannahs. Among their numbers are species of reedbuck, kob, puku and waterbuck, wildebeest, impala, Arabian oryx, and sable antelope. Grazing antelopes are medium- to large-sized animals, some of which have distinctive and diagnostic horns. These range from long and straight (gemsbok) to long and curved (sable antelope).

The most widespread and familiar of the grazing antelopes in central and southern Africa is the impala. Recognized by the black thigh spot on the flanks, these reddish-brown animals live in groups of 50 or more individuals in open savannah woodland. Like many other African species, the birth of young is usually timed to coincide with the seasonal rains, enabling the impala to take full advantage of the resulting new plant growth.

The sable antelope has gracefully curved horns that give the species a striking appearance. The horns are larger in males than females but gain stature with age in both genders.

Several species of grazing antelopes are threatened by human activities. Competition with domesticated animals, often other ruminants, for grazing and water is a problem, while hunting is a threat to certain arid-terrain species. The Arabian oryx, for example, became extinct in the wild, although the species has been reintroduced to Oman from captive-bred stock. The addax, an elegant, pale antelope from the Sahara is also in dire peril.

A rich supply of mother's milk keeps this young Beisa oryx well fed in the early stages of its life. Although dependent upon its mother for food, it was able to keep up with an adult on the run within a few days of being born.

A select number of African antelopes have made wetlands and lake margins their domain. This common waterbuck has a yellow-billed stork as a companion, the bird stabbing at fish and amphibians disturbed by the antelope's progress.

Gazelles and Their Relatives

Among the 30 species that comprise this varied subfamily are representatives from Mongolia, India, Arabia, and Africa. Most gazelles are animals of open, grassy country, but some of their relatives, the klipspringer and the dik-dik, favor different terrain. The former is found around rocky outcrops, while the latter inhabits dense cover.

True gazelles are graceful, elegant animals with comparatively slender bodies and long legs and necks. Most are capable of considerable speeds on level ground and some, notably the springbok, are renowned for pronking: alternation of high-speed running with vertical leaps.

The so-called dwarf antelopes—relatives of gazelles—are, as their name suggests, usually small. In general, they favor denser cover than their larger cousins and tend to be solitary, territorial animals. In addition to the klipspringer and dik-dik, the group includes the royal antelope and the steenbok.

The ability to run at speed is an attribute vital to the survival of this Thomson's gazelle. A healthy animal can outrun most predators, and only the cheetah is fast enough to catch this species in pursuit on level ground.

The need to drink has lured this springbok to a water hole to drink. A visit by a solitary animal is comparatively unusual because, like many other antelopes, the species finds safety in numbers.

The Kirk's dik-dik is one of the smallest of Africa's antelopes. Pairs of these charming animals maintain territories in the dense cover of savannah scrub, where they mark the boundaries with scent.

Goat Antelopes

Distribution of the goat antelopes is essentially restricted to the Northern Hemisphere. Representatives from among the subfamily's 26 species occur in southern Asia, southern Europe, northern Africa, and northern North America. Almost without exception, the goat antelopes are animals of challenging habitats. The majority live on steep and rugged mountain terrain, although one species, the saiga, lives in the Mongolian desert, enduring searing heat in summer and bitter cold in winter. There is even a species, the musk ox, that is a permanent resident in the high Arctic, while at the other extreme, the serow resides in tropical forests of Southeast Asia.

The goat antelopes include the ancestors of two of our most important domesticated animals. Domestic goats are derived from the wild goats that still roam crags in parts of southeastern Europe and western Asia, while the mouflon is the ancestor of domestic sheep.

As a group, the goat antelopes are robust and compact animals with powerful legs and feet, ideally suited to climbing and running on rough, broken ground. The males of many species develop huge and impressive horns as they age.

Some goat antelope species have massively developed horns that make them among the most impressive animals in their home terrain. Bighorn sheep are arguably the most imposing representatives of the group in North America, with males developing huge spiral horns, which they use to good effect in competition with rivals. In the Old World, they find their counterparts in ibex-type species. The ibex is represented by scattered populations in mountainous and rugged desert areas; each species differs from the others in subtle ways. Thus, the Alpine ibex is generally larger and heavier than the Nubian ibex, and the two populations will never interbreed without human intervention. In the Iberian peninsula, large-horned goat antelopes are represented by the Spanish ibex, which is widespread in the Pyrenees mountains.

In addition to these large-horned goat antelopes, the mountains of Europe and North America also have smaller, less-endowed representatives. In the Old World, chamois are nimble-footed inhabitants of the Pyrenees, Alps, and Caucasus mountains, while in the Rocky Mountains, the elegant mountain goat, with its thick, white coat and short, sharp horns, is found. In mountain goats, the horns are definitely not for show, and bloody battles often end with their white coats splattered with red. Hardiest of all North America's mountain-goat antelopes is Dall's sheep, which lives in Alaska and northern British Columbia, preferring terrain that is hostile in both summer and winter.

As with other ruminants, chewing the cud is part of everyday life for this Dall's sheep. The process can just as well be undertaken lying down as standing up.

The musk ox is a permanent resident of the high Arctic, and its thick coat allows it to survive the prolonged winter with indifference. The animal's massive horns and its habit of forming defensive rings when attacked make the species invulnerable to all but the most concerted attacks by predators.

*Mountain goats,
where they still
occur, are true
masters of the
North American
mountain ranges.
Even when the
ground is covered
with ice and
snow, these sure-
footed creatures
negotiate the
most seemingly
inaccessible
crags without
hesitation.*

FEEDING AND DEFENSE

With the exception of a few species of mouse deer that are known to take small animals as part of their diets, all ruminants are essentially herbivores. The range of habitat preferences and precise diet vary considerably across the group, but whatever their shape, size, or geographical location, all ruminants show certain adaptations that suit their lifestyle. Some of these are structural and functional adaptations, while others are behavioral in nature.

Rumination

The dentition—the arrangement and character of the teeth—of almost all ruminants conforms to a basic plan that differs in many key respects to the standard mammalian structure. There are three premolar and three molar teeth on each side of the upper and lower jaws. Their surfaces are generally molded into convoluted ridges to assist the grinding of plant food, with the orientation of the opposing surfaces so arranged that sideways jaw movements become extremely efficient. The upper incisor teeth are absent and so are the upper canines, except in the mouse deer and musk deer, where they are extremely conspicuous. In all ruminants, the lower canines are similar in appearance to the incisors alongside which they sit. All eight teeth at the front edge of the lower jaw serve the function of opposing the thickened upper lip so that vegetation can be torn either from the ground or from a branch.

Having ingested vegetation, ruminants are faced with the problem of extracting nutritional value from cellulose plant fibers, a material that is resistant to the digestive enzymes of conventional mammalian systems. To overcome this problem, they have evolved a multichambered stomach in one part of which bacterial fermentation takes place. Once complete, the fermented mass is regurgitated and macerated—commonly called

Accidents associated with combat are rare among rutting elk stags, but the potential is certainly there for one of the sharp-tipped branches to inflict considerable damage to an opponent.

In northern latitudes, the first snows of winter often fall before the leaves have completely fallen from the trees. This mule deer is determined to take advantage of the few remaining aspen leaves, even though it gets a dusting of snow as it does so.

chewing the cud—after which it is swallowed again and digested in a more typical fashion, using the digestive juices of a different chamber of the stomach.

Grazers and Browsers

Most deer are essentially grazing animals, although a little browsing may be done by some species. Grasses are an essential part of the diet for many, but for deer in northern temperate regions, experiencing four distinct seasons, this food is generally only available during spring and summer. At other times of year, they are forced to switch to alternative

food sources such as fruit, nuts, and browsed evergreen shrubs.

The diet of caribou and reindeer—the deer that live at the mostly northerly latitudes of all—remains fairly constant throughout the year despite dramatic changes in temperature and the layer of snow and ice that blankets the Arctic in winter. They feed on reindeer moss—actually a type of lichen—gaining access to this food in winter by using their hooves and antlers to scrape away the snow. With the coming of spring, the flush of willow leaves and herbaceous arctic plants are exploited to the full.

It often comes as a great surprise to people visiting wilderness areas of northern North America to discover just how amphibious moose are during the summer months. Although they certainly gain respite from biting flies by spending much of their time immersed in pools and lakes, the main reason they do it is to feed on aquatic vegetation, which is rich in sodium. At other times of year they are forced to feed on grasses or subsist on the foliage and shoots of more shrubby plants.

Arguably, the greatest extremes in food and feeding methods are seen among African ruminants. As in most other parts of the world, grasses play an important part in the diet of many species, although adaptations have

allowed different species to exploit subtly different niches, thus avoiding undue competition. Many antelope species favor lush grasslands, while wildebeests, on the other hand, feed on extremely short turf, including that previously grazed by other ruminants. African buffalo and waterbuck live partly amphibious lives, grazing wetland vegetation, while species of oryx are adapted to live in near-desert environments.

In African savannah grasslands, many of the varied ruminant species spread themselves out and feed on subtly different areas of vegetation. Separation of feeding niches is not always simply a matter of temporal spacing, however, and once in a while, different ruminants feed alongside one another in apparent harmony. With the gerenuk, the way in which competition with other ruminants is avoided is immediately obvious:

They have evolved a long neck and an ability to stand confidently on their hind legs. This enables them to feed on shrub foliage out of reach to all other antelope species. Going one stage further, the giraffe feeds on levels of foliage out of reach of all other animals.

Defensive Weapons

The vast majority of ruminant species have skulls topped with bony outgrowths for at least part of the year. Depending on the way in which these outgrowths form and whether they are permanent or seasonal, they are described as either antlers or horns. They are most frequently seen in male animals but occur in females of some species, too. Horns and antlers serve a variety of functions, notably in display and in intraspecies disputes, but they can also help with feeding and defense against predators.

In the antelope world, few sights are more comical than that of a gerenuk teetering on its hind legs while grazing the acacia scrub. Although this antic may look slightly ungainly, it does enable this species to exploit vegetation out of reach to almost all of its cousins.

Using his long legs for wading, this bull moose is feasting on submerged vegetation growing in the clear waters of this arctic pool. A red-necked (northern) phalarope accompanies his progress, catching insects disturbed by his actions.

Scimitar-horned oryx are adapted to arid terrain on the fringes of the Sahara Desert in North Africa. Their beautifully curved horns are among the most elegant of any horned animal; despite their slender appearance, they are strong and lethally sharp.

Horns

Horns are skull outgrowths that are present for life and that increase in size as an animal ages. They vary in shape from simple and straight to curved and ridged, while ranging in size from the insignificant to the immense and almost cumbersome.

Of all the horned animals, the giraffe has perhaps the least prominent horns, particularly in proportion to the size of the animal itself. They are proportionately short and stubby and—uniquely among ruminants—are covered with a permanent layer of skin and adorned with tufts of black hair at the tips. Giraffes also differ from their relatives by being born with horns, albeit ones in a reduced and compressed state. The horns continue to grow throughout life and are larger in males than females; the former also develop additional hornlike outgrowths from the skull as they age. Males use their horns in head-butting competitions with one another.

The North American pronghorn is unusual in having bony horns that are covered in a layer of black skin that is shed each year after the rut. In male animals, the horns develop backward-pointing hooked tips. Pronghorns are unique among horned animals in general because in males, at least, the horns branch and form forward-pointing projections, giving them the appearance of the antlers of a young male deer.

In common with those of sheep, goats, and antelopes, the horns of wild cattle and their relatives comprise a solid core of bone over which a layer of keratin, the horn proper, grows. Keratin is the same material from which hair and fingernails are made. Horns are retained for life and continue to grow as the animal ages; as a general rule, males have larger horns than females of the same species.

In some species of wild cattle and their relatives, the horns are rather insignificant, although in the majority of cases, they become

Bouts of head butting between rival bighorn sheep rams can be a draining and seemingly painful experience. In a prelude to this behavior, ritualized dominance displays known as "bowing" sometimes establish elements of the hierarchy without the need to resort to force.

extremely prominent. The horns are no mere adornments, and in the case of the North American bison, they are used by males to gore one another during the annual rut—if the animal is given half a chance by his opponent. Horns of the African buffalo grow to immense proportions, effectively tripling the width of bull's head when viewed face on. It is no wonder then that this species is generally perceived as being the most dangerous African mammal for humans, charging and occasionally

Unusual for horned animals, the horns of the pronghorn are often branched. They are larger, and the forward-pointing projections more conspicuous in males than females.

During the rutting season, fights among bull North American bison become common. Most involve head-to-head pushing contests, but occasionally the sharp-tipped horns are used to inflict severe injuries on opponents.

disemboweling intruders at the slightest provocation. The species is effectively invulnerable to all predators except lions or people armed with weapons, and its defense is undoubtedly enhanced by the fact that it lives in herds.

In one group of wild cattle relatives, the so-called spiral-horned antelopes, the horns are especially elegantly proportioned. Greater kudu males, for example, have a near-perfect and symmetrical twist to their horns, which can have an overall length of 30 inches (80 centimeters) or more. Female greater kudu lack horns.

Like those of almost all other horned animals, the horns of antelopes and gazelles are unbranched, but the array of shapes and sizes they exhibit is extraordinary. They range from short to immense; are often ridged and sometimes keeled; and can be straight, curved forward, curved backward, or spiral. Most male antelopes and gazelles have horns, and females of some species possess them, too. In males, they are often used in interlocking battles with other males where both attempt to assert their

dominance and win the right to mate with females. Presumably they also serve as visual flags of a male's prowess: the larger the horns, the fitter the animal in biological terms. It is assumed that in species where females have horns, they are used to defend areas of good feeding against other individuals in the group.

The most remarkable examples of horns can be found among certain species of goats and sheep. Ibex from the mountains of Europe and Asia and bighorn sheep from North America are perhaps the classic examples, and as with most of their relatives, males have larger horns than females of the same age; these increase in size as the animal ages. The massive horn size that is achieved in mature males reflects their importance in battles for dominance. These horns are definitely not just for show, as anyone who has witnessed the head-bashing disputes of these animals can testify. The urge to do battle, or at least to rehearse for dramas later in life, appears at an early age; surprisingly young ibexes, for example, can be seen fighting on the precarious slopes they inhabit.

From an early age, mountain goat kids are as indifferent as their parents to the forbidding, mountainous habitats in which they find themselves. The death-defying speed with which they negotiate almost sheer crags can often leave the observer feeling giddy and panic-stricken, although for the goats this is all part of everyday life.

Male greater kudu are resplendent with magnificent spiral-shaped horns. As well as reflecting an animal's stature compared to potential rivals, these adornments are formidable weapons of defense.

As a prelude to the autumn rut, these male ibexes practice the skills needed for the challenges to come. With horns interlocked, they try to force one another into a retreat and establish a hierarchy among the strongest individuals.

35

Unlike the antlers found in deer, horns are present for life and grow with age. Except where damage has occurred, they show a remarkable degree of symmetry as can be seen in those borne by this red hartebeest from Namibia.

The huge eland is a spiral-horned antelope, more closely related to wild cattle than to true antelopes. It occurs in several different races across its sub-Saharan range and favors areas of open grassland.

Antlers

Antlers are seen in males of most species of deer. Reindeer and caribou are the only members of the group in which they are present in females, too. In common with horns, antlers are outgrowths from the skull, but they differ in several fundamental respects. They are grown and shed on an annual basis and are produced from the layer of skin that shrouds them. As a consequence, a fully formed antler is made up entirely of bone with no horn, or keratin, present.

The growing antlers are nourished by the layer of skin, known as velvet, that covers them. When they are fully grown, the skin is typically shed just prior to the start of the rutting season. In most species the antlers are shed generally after breeding has finished, and not infrequently, they are eaten by the animal that dropped them, providing

Mature caribou bulls possess superb sets of antlers that are used to good effect in the rutting season. Uniquely among deer, female caribou also possess antlers, and it is presumed that these aid in foraging for food in snowy conditions.

As a prelude to mating, a bull moose courts a female, sniffing her to see whether she is in heat or not. Only the male moose has the characteristic antlers, shaped like outstretched hands.

Following page: White-tailed deer, along with many of their relatives, often engage in fraying tree bark with their antlers. In most species, this behavior helps remove the velvet surrounding newly grown antlers, but for some, it also is a method of marking territory.

a valuable source of calcium and other minerals. New antlers begin to grow again soon after the loss of the previous set, leaving the deer without antlers of one size or another for only a brief period each year. Antlers become successively bigger and more complex in their division with each year's growth.

The largest antlers are seen in the moose, and arguably the most complex are found in caribou, reindeer, and red deer. Males of all deer species use their antlers to do combat with one another during the rutting season. The fact that reindeer females also possess antlers may reflect their usefulness as tools for scraping away snow cover on the ground.

When deer antlers are fully formed, they shed the coating of skin, or "velvet," that covers them while they are growing. This caribou has recently lost its velvet, leaving its antlers stained bloodred.

Although they are destined to become rivals at maturity, these young buck white-tailed deer are engaged in seemingly affectionate, mutual grooming in a sunny woodland clearing.

FOUR ADAPTATIONS

The similarities and differences among ruminants can be learned by considering four familiar animals: caribou, white-tailed deer, wildebeests, and mountain goats. Each has evolved strategies for survival, enabling it to adjust to the vagaries of the weather, terrain, and food sources of its habitat.

The Caribou

The winter months are a time of great hardship for the caribou, whose habitat stretches across the northern latitudes of the North American continent. For much of the period from late October to February, the ground is frozen hard, and snow often blankets the landscape. The animals grow a thick winter coat, which helps fend off the worst of the winter chill, but finding enough food to eat is a real problem. The powerful, hoofed feet are used to scrape away the snow to expose the meager rations of grass and moss that lie underneath. On occasion, the caribou also use their antlers for this purpose, although males have generally shed these by December. Females do not lose their antlers until February and so gain a few weeks extra use out of these organic ice picks.

Spring is slow to arrive in the subarctic lands on which the caribou spend the winter. In March, however, there are signs of a thaw, and the deer themselves have begun to grow restless. Just as bursting buds herald the change of seasons, so too does the appearance of newly forming sets of antlers on the heads of the caribou. By early May, new plant growth is everywhere to be seen, and the caribou begin their long northward spring migration, feasting on the lush supply of grasses and willow leaves.

The caribou generally reach their arctic summering grounds in July, at which time the females give birth to their calves. Within a few hours of birth, the calves can walk, and within a few weeks they can keep up with the herd on the move. The adult caribou feed voraciously at this time of year, building up their reserves for times of hardship to come. Diet is important to the females because, until weaned, the calves depend on having well-fed mothers. For the males, the diet can have a strong bearing on whether or not they are able to mate in the weeks to come.

By a miracle of timing, the colors of the caribou's tundra habitat become most vivid just as the autumn rut begins. Males spend much of their time competing with one another for the right to mate with the females; this leaves little time for them to feed.

By early summer, caribou have reached the final stage of their northward migration. Here they feed on the comparatively lush tundra vegetation and build up reserves in preparation for the autumn rut.

The spring and autumn migrations undertaken by North America's caribou herds often involve long treks through snowy terrain. Not only is progress impeded by the frozen landscape, but feeding becomes difficult as well.

During the summer months, the caribou herds are constantly on the move, searching for new and better grazing. Given the nature of the summer arctic landscape, their wanderings invariably necessitate crossing rivers and lakes. Immersion in water brings temporary relief from the biting insects.

The rutting season takes place in September and October, when males battle one another for the right to maintain a territory through which the females wander at will in search of grazing. Female caribou are not automatically loyal to any single patch of ground and need vigorous encouragement on the part of the male to remain in his territory long enough to mate. The whole exhausting process goes on for several weeks but is brought to a close abruptly with the first flurries of snow. With the threat of winter looming, the caribou herds migrate south again. Needless to say, having to battle with rivals and keep a constant eye on the whereabouts of females leaves the male caribou with little time to feed. By this time a number of males are in an exhausted and poorly nourished state, and many succumb during the long march south when the herds cover hundreds of miles and sometimes more than a thousand.

In the dead of winter, with the vegetation often buried under several feet of snow, feeding becomes a struggle for caribou. The hooves and antlers then come into their own and are often used to expose the hidden mosses and lichens.

The White-Tailed Deer

The white-tailed deer is a charming native of the Americas, with its heaviest distribution in Canada and with sizable populations across the United States, except in parts of the Southwest. It is also found from Mexico to Peru and northeastern Brazil. Living in a variety of habitats, these deer prefer woodlands that offer only enough foliage for concealment and therefore are rarely found in densely forested areas.

They are both grazers and browsers and feed on a variety of foods that include grasses, shrubs, twigs, nuts, lichens, and mushrooms. Their preferred feeding times are the hours around sunrise and sunset. In the fall, white-tails living in mountainous regions move to lower areas where food is more plentiful and easier to find during the winter.

The white-tailed deer is not a herd animal but, instead, is rather solitary. The typical family group consists of a female (doe), her yearling daughter, and the newly born fawn or fawns. The males (bucks) live either alone or in small groups. The only time of the year when the sexes may mingle, except for mating, is

For the first few months of its life, this young white-tailed deer will remain in the company of its mother and be the subject of her ever-watchful gaze. Unlike its mother, the fawn is generally oblivious to the possible dangers of everyday life.

Deer shed their antlers annually during the winter. As they grow back in the spring, their size and complexity increases, adding additional "points." This white-tailed deer is a 10-point buck.

Unlike adults, the young of mule deer, and of many other species, have spotted coats. The markings afford the youngsters superb camouflage, especially during the first few days of life when they remain motionless in the undergrowth.

during the winter, when bucks and does of all ages happen to come together in areas where food is available.

In the colder months, white-tailed deer have brownish gray coats that allow them to blend remarkably well with the rather somber colors of the leafless woodlands. Yearling animals can still be distinguished from adults by their smaller size, but differentiating the sexes of the adults at this season can be difficult because males begin shedding their antlers in January and do not grow new ones until at least April. Winter is a particularly important time for the females: Because mating takes place in the autumn, beginning in October, gestation, or development of the embryo, occurs during this season. Pregnancy lasts between six and a half and seven months, allowing the birth of fawns to begin in April. Females experiencing

Autumn is a time of plenty for these white-tailed deer. However, the vibrant colors of the woodland herald the imminent arrival of a change to wintry, less abundant conditions.

their first pregnancy usually give birth to a single fawn and then to two or more in subsequent seasons.

Early spring sees a flush of new growth in the woodlands, and the tender young buds and shoots make a welcome change from the deer's winter diet. These also enable the females to produce nourishing milk for their newborns. For the first few days of their lives, the fawns remain motionless in the undergrowth while the female is off feeding, returning periodically to suckle her young. Even though they can move about after three weeks, the fawns stay close to their mother as she goes about her daily routine. During the summer, adult white-tailed deer have reddish-brown coats, much richer than the winter counterpart. However, the fawns' coats are spotted, affording superb camouflage amid the dappled vegetation.

The rutting season for whitetails is in the autumn, usually reaching its height during November. Males spar with each other in ritualistic confrontations to determine not the domination of a territory or a group of females but the right to mate with a particular doe. The winner then stays with the doe until mating occurs.

In the last days of summer and during the early autumn, the deer spend much of their time feeding on the bountiful supply of vegetation that is still available. At this time, the darker winter coat replaces the brighter hued one of summer for both adults and youngsters. The hairs of these coats are notably thick, providing the vital warmth needed to ensure the survival of these hardy animals through the months of winter to come.

Throughout the November rut, this buck white-tailed deer is likely to take great exception to the presence of any rival male nearby. However, because this 8-month-old fawn is no threat to the buck, it is treated with a degree of tolerance not shown to animals 2 years its elder.

The Wildebeest

Despite the fact that wildebeests are classified as antelopes, these strange-looking creatures still resemble, at first glance, a bizarre cross between a bison and a horse. The species occurs widely across the grassy plains of eastern and southern Africa and is generally found in vast herds. Given their prodigious appetites and the fickle and often seasonal nature of the grasslands of this continent, most populations follow the rains in search of fresh grazing in a rather nomadic fashion. Wildebeests that live in East Africa undertake perhaps the best-known and most firmly established of these migrations, a journey that takes them on an annual tour across two of the region's best-known wildlife areas, the Serengeti Plain in Tanzania and the Masai Mara in Kenya.

On the equator, the cycle of seasons, experienced in the Northern Hemisphere, does not occur. Instead of temperature changes, there are dry and rainy seasons, with the annual rains causing new vegetation to spring to life.

December sees the wildebeest herds firmly established on their feeding grounds at the southern end of the Serengeti Plain, where the rains of the previous autumn have induced a fresh growth of grass. Through judicious timing, this period of relative plenty coincides with the peak period for female wildebeests to give birth. Thanks to modern filming, many people have viewed this spectacle for themselves, along with the amazing sight of a young calf getting to its feet minutes after being born. Despite the fact that the calves start to eat grass when just a few weeks old, they continue to suckle their mothers for up to 8 months.

Throughout the months of February, March, and April, the herds roam rather aimlessly and nomadically across the southern Serengeti until May and June, when the annual rut takes place. During brief pauses in the wanderings of the herd, male wildebeests establish and defend temporary territories through which female members of the herd pass from time to time, only to be courted and mated.

Very little rain falls at this time of year, and the ground becomes parched and dry. As the grass withers in the drought, so the

Despite their size and the speed at which they can run, wildebeests feature strongly in the diet of lions because these big cats are specialists at ambushing prey. A single wildebeest kill is likely to satisfy a lion pride for several days, unless interloping hyenas manage to assert control over the carcass.

Despite the ravening jaws of crocodiles, the majority of wildebeests that embark on a crossing of the Mara River survive their trial. After staggering onto dry land, their ordeal does not end, however, because they must watch for predators lying in ambush for them.

wildebeests' interest in mating diminishes. The herds gradually coalesce and move steadily northwestward toward Lake Victoria. By July and early August, the need to find grazing of some sort drives them onward into the Masai Mara, the herds crossing one major obstacle, the Mara River, to achieve their goal. Many succumb to the waiting jaws of crocodiles and the ambushes of lions, but enough survive to reach new feeding grounds. Autumn rains herald the start of the return trip of more than 100 miles, which takes the wildebeests back across the Mara River and south to the Serengeti Plain.

The Bighorn Sheep

Bighorn sheep live in some of the most remote and inhospitable parts of North America, favoring landscapes that on a good day, can also be among the most breathtakingly stunning. The species occurs primarily across the western half of the continent, down the spine of the Rocky Mountains south to northern Mexico.

Precipitous cliffs and crags are classic terrain for bighorn sheep, and so sparse is the meager vegetation supported by these habitats that it is often a wonder what such large animals can possibly find to eat. The advantage gained by living in such a hostile environment comes at least partly from the bighorn's ability to avoid and escape from danger. Few other animals are nimble and sure-footed enough to follow a herd of bighorn sheep, the animals soft foot pads absorbing the impact of their death-defying leaps and climbs.

Seasonal rains in Tanzania's Serengeti National Park have promoted a lush growth of vegetation that in turn, feeds the herds of wildebeest that migrate there each year around Christmas. Most of the calves are born at that time.

A front view of this male bighorn sheep reveals the degree to which the skull is thickened at the base of the horns. As a result of the strengthening and padding, rams seem unmoved by the blows they inflict on one another in head-butting contests.

The annual migration undertaken by East African wildebeests involves crossing the Mara River close to the border of Kenya with Tanzania. The animals are understandably hesitant about entering the water because it is the domain of sizable crocodiles.

Following page: When two rival males find that they are evenly matched in size and horn stature, the only way to settle a dispute over hierarchy is to do battle. These head-butting contests cannot easily result in lasting damage to the animals. However, anyone watching and hearing such a spectacle would find this fact hard to believe.

This trio of bighorn sheep rams may appear to be strolling aimlessly and enjoying one another's company. The reality is that they are assessing each other's relative biological fitness as a prelude to the autumn rut.

females and young, and the herds gradually move to lower altitudes as the season progresses and the weather worsens.

The massive, curved horns of male bighorns come into their own during the rutting season, which lasts for much of November and December. Using the females' scent as a guide, the male keeps a close check on whether or not they are in heat. However, he is seldom alone in his scrutiny of the herd, and head-butting competitions between males of similar stature are common. Typically, the dominant male tries to place himself uphill of his opponent before hurling himself toward his rival. For human onlookers, these head-to-head clashes are painful to watch and sound as though real damage is being inflicted. Fortunately for the sheep, their skulls are cushioned and strengthened to absorb the shock of the impact. If there is a large discrepancy between the potential sparring partners, the smaller of the two usually retreats gracefully, and they seldom come to blows.

For much of the year, bighorn sheep are essentially gregarious animals, although during the spring and summer at least, the animals separate themselves into single-sex herds. When the young are born in May or June, they remain in the company of their mothers. Just prior to the rutting season, which begins in late autumn and early winter, the males usually join the

During the comparatively lazy days of summer, bighorn sheep tend to form single-sex flocks. This group of rams, in Canada's Jasper National Park, seem thoroughly at ease with one another; this tolerance will disappear as the rutting season approaches.

The fearless way in which bighorn sheep negotiate the rocky crags and cliffs, on which they spend much of their lives, stands them in good stead in other, equally challenging terrain. This animal is about to cross a raging torrent, leaping from stone to stone with total confidence.

OBSERVING ANIMALS

Fortunately for the mammal enthusiast, most wild ruminants are medium- to large-sized animals, and their discovery is usually relatively straightforward. Getting close and prolonged views of them is, however, sometimes more a challenge. While many are indifferent to human observers, a few are wary. Some live in habitats, such as forests, in which observation is difficult, and a few favor sites such as precipitous and dangerous mountains and cliffs.

Despite the challenge presented by a few species, the range of opportunities for studying ruminants is unsurpassed among mammals, and the thrill of watching the more challenging species adds spice to the study of this fascinating group. As an added bonus, all continents except Australia and Antarctica have naturally occurring species of ruminants. The following is a guide to some of the best sites for their observation.

North America

Two species of deer are widespread and common enough in North America not to need specific sites. These are the mule deer, sometimes called black-tailed deer, which occurs across the western half of the continent, and the white-tailed deer, which is much more widespread although absent from parts of the Southwest. The distribution of both species continues northward almost to the limit of the tree line.

Although the sika deer has its origins in Asia, the species was introduced to Britain and today can be found both in deer parks and as feral populations in certain parts of southern England. The animal's coat changes with the seasons, from orange-brown in summer to a much darker hue in winter.

An immense bull moose surveys his tundra domain. The tattered remains of velvet can be seen trailing from the fingerlike points that fringe his spreading, flattened antlers.

Mountain goats have stocky, muscular bodies. The legs are especially powerful and allow the animal to leap and run with speed and confidence on terrifyingly steep and broken terrain. As a consequence, there are few places inaccessible to these amazing animals.

Arguably, the best national park in the United States for watching ruminants is Yellowstone. In addition to mule deer and whitetails, wapati, moose, pronghorn, bison, and bighorn sheep can be seen. A visit during the summer months, July to September, may coincide with the rutting season of the bison, when the spectacle of rival bulls bellowing and head butting occurs. For northern specialties, Alaska's Denali National Park offers caribou, moose, and Dall's sheep; the main rutting season for moose and caribou is in September and October, when the colors of the tundra vegetation are at their finest.

During the autumn rut, the bugling calls of bull elk echo through aspen groves in the foothills of the Rocky Mountains. If an obvious size difference exists between two bulls, the intimidating calls of the larger animal are usually sufficient to drive away the rival.

Few places offer better opportunities for seeing caribou than Alaska's Denali National Park. A visit in the autumn has the added attraction of the tundra, which assumes its seasonal hues of gold and red.

Europe

Roe deer live throughout mainland Europe, though absent from the Mediterranean region. They are fairly easy to observe in woodland terrain. The red deer requires more open country, and its distribution is scattered across Europe. It can be seen to particularly good advantage in Scotland in the Cairngorms region of the Highlands, which offers the added bonus of roe deer as well as a feral population of reindeer. Because it is so thinly scattered, the fallow deer is perhaps easiest to see in southern England. European bison can be found in Bialowieza National Park in Poland, while mouflon is perhaps best seen on Cyprus, where a mountain refuge has been established for it.

Chamois are widespread in many European mountain ranges, but ibexes are decidedly patchy in distribution. The best place to see them is in Gran Paradiso National Park in the Italian Alps.

In a collective frenzy, these male Spanish ibex are battering one another in an attempt to determine some form of hierarchy. Although still persecuted, the species is locally common in parts of the Pyrenees mountain range.

"Look but do not touch" is the rule when a human discovers a young deer. If handled, this baby roe deer will become tainted with human scent, and there is a real risk that the mother will subsequently abandon it.

Africa

For the mammal watcher, Africa is a paradise. Here are found the largest living land animals, elephants and rhinos, as well as big cats, monkeys, and apes. These fascinate the first-time visitor, who then notices the vast numbers of other animals. Within Africa's huge game reserves and national parks, immense herds of game animals can be seen, an amazing number of which are ruminants.

In Kenya's Amboseli National Park and the Masai Mara Game Reserve and in neighboring Tanzania's Serengeti National Park, vast numbers of wildebeest and impala can be seen along with smaller aggregations of species such as giraffes, Thomson's and Grant's gazelles, topi, Coke's hartebeest, waterbuck, and dik-dik.

Waterbuck are easy to see in many of East Africa's game reserves and national parks. Here at Samburu in Kenya, these two animals are engaging in playful sparring, a useful training exercise for real competition.

The delightfully named bongo is adorned with superb colors and patterns, particularly those on the face. Seen out of context, these markings attract our attention, but in its natural haunts, the mountain forests of Africa, they afford the animal superb camouflage in the dappled light.

Beisa oryx are arguably the most elegant of all the antelopes to grace Kenya's Samburu Game Reserve. Their incredibly long horns, which make identification an easy matter, are used as potentially lethal weapons when defending against predators.

This herd of impala is keeping a wary eye on a passing leopard. Although they have most to fear from this predator after dark, the possibility of a surprise daytime attack can never be ruled out.

A relative of the ibex, the markhor is best known for its extraordinary spiral horns, which are most pronounced in males. The species prefers wooded mountain slopes and is found in areas ranging from Afghanistan to northern India. However it is generally scarce and wary as a result of human persecution.

Asia

For the animal lover, Asia lacks the spectacle of numbers offered by many regions of Africa, and its ruminants are seldom so easy to see. Nevertheless, here there are species found nowhere else in the world.

The foothills of the Himalayas in the northern Indian province of Ladakh sometimes yield sightings of markhor (a relative of the ibex), argalis (a relative of the mouflon), and blue sheep. At lower altitudes in Nepal, there are sambar, Indian muntjac, hog deer, and spotted deer or chital, while gaur (the Asian bison) is seen at Royal Chitwan National Park. Kanha National Park in India offers swamp deer, sambar, and spotted deer along with the site's other main attraction, the tiger.

Fortunately, the distant and exotic locations described above are not the only wild places where these impressive mammals can be seen. With patience and planning, a few horned or antlered animals can be found in wooded and mountainous areas in almost any part of the world, even near large urban centers. In fact, in certain locales the populations of some species are on the increase after years of decline. There is hope, therefore, that humans will be able to continue to enjoy glimpses of these beautiful and gentle wild creatures for many years to come.

The chital or spotted deer is widespread in India and is easy to see in many of the country's national parks. Although generally tolerant of human observers, the animals have good reason to be wary of other threats because the species is a favorite prey of the tiger

The extraordinary takin comes from western China as well as neighboring Bhutan and Burma. The species is renowned for its odor because the skin of almost the entire body secretes a powerfully pungent oily substance.

INDEX

*Page numbers in **bold-face** type indicate photo captions.*

INDEX (continued)

markhor, 70, **70**
Masai Mara Game Reserve, Kenya, 52, 55, 67
moose, 10
 antlers, 10, **10**, **39**, 42, **61**
 diet and feeding habits, 28, **28**, **31**
 in Europe, 10
 observing, 62
mouflon, 22, 64, 70
mountain goats, 22, **23**, **34**, 45, **62**
mouse deer, 7, 27
mule deer (black-tailed deer), 11-12, **12**, **27**, **50**
 observing, 61, 62
muntjacs, 10, 12
 Indian, 70
musk, 10
musk deer, 7, 10, **27**
musk ox, 22, 22

nilgai, 16
North American bison, 15, 16, **16**, **28**, **33**, 62
 horns, 33, **33**
North American pronghorn, 15, **15**, 33, **33**
North American ruminants
 bovids, 15, 22, **23**, 34, 55
 deer species, 10, 11-12, **12**, 45, 61
 observing, 61-62, **63**
Northern Hemisphere, goat antelopes, 22
Nubian ibex, 22

okapi, 15
Old World goat antelopes, 22
Oman, 19
oryxes, 30
 Arabian, 19
 Beisa, **19**, **67**
 scimitar-horned, **31**

phalerope, 31
pigs, 7
pronghorn, 15, **15**
 horns, **15**, 33, **33**
 observing, 62
pronking, 20
puku, 19

Pyrenees, 22, **64**

red deer, **4**, 11, **11**, 42
 habitats and distribution, 11, 12, 64
 North American counterpart. *See*
 (wapiti (elk)
red hartebeest, **36**
reedbuck, 19
reindeer, 28, 39, 42, 64
reindeer moss, 28
reticulated giraffe, 15, **15**
rhinoceroses, 7
Rocky Mountain ruminants. *See*
 bighorn sheep; mountain goats; wapiti
roe deer, 64, **64**
royal antelope, 20
Royal Chitwan National Park, Nepal, 70
ruminants, 3-4
 amphibious, 28, 30
 classification and family divisions, 7-22
 dentition, 27
 diets, 27, 28-29
 digestive system, 4, 7, 27-28
 observing, 61-70
rumination, 7, 27-28
rut
 bighorn sheep, 58, **58**
 combat during, 42. *See also* head-butting contests
 deer species, **4**, **7**, **10**, 11, **12**, **27**, **39**, **47**, 51, **51**, 62, **62**, **64**
 musk deer, 10
 North American bison, 33, **33**, 62
 and velvet shedding, 39
 wildebeest, 52

sable antelope, 19, **19**
Sahara Desert, 19, **31**, **36**
saiga, 22
sambar, 70
Samburu Game Reserve, Kenya, **67**
Serengeti National Park, Tanzania, **55**, 67
Serengeti Plain, Tanzania, 52, 55
serow, 22
sheep, 3, 7
 bighorn, 22, **23**, **33**, 34, **55**, 55-58, **58**

blue, 70
Dall's, **4**, 22, **22**, 62
domesticated, 3, 22
head-butting contests, **4**, **33**
horns, 3, 33, 34
sika deer, **61**
sitatunga, 16
Spanish ibex, 22, **64**
spiral-horned antelopes, 16, 34
 eland, 16, **36**
spotted deer (chital), 70, **70**
springbok, 20, **20**
steenbok, 20
swamp deer, 70

takin, **70**
Thomson's gazelle, **20**, 67
topi, 67

ungulates, 7

velvet, 39, **39**, **42**, **61**

wapiti, 11
 European counterpart. *See* red deer
 North American (elk), **7**, 11, **27**, 62, **62**
waterbuck, 19, **19**, 30
 observing, 67, 67
water buffalo, 15, 16
water chevrotain, 7
white-tailed deer, 7, 11-12, **28**, **42**, 45, 48-51, **50**, **51**
 antlers, **39**, **48**, 50
 diet and feeding habits, 48
 observing, 61, 62
 reproduction, 50-51
 young (fawns), **48**, 51, **51**
wild cattle and relatives, 15-16, 33. *See also* bison; buffalo; kudu
wildebeests, 19, 45, 52-55, **52**, **53**, **55**
 feeding habits, 30, 52, **55**
 observing, 67

yak, 16
Yellowstone National Park, **28**, 62

FURTHER READING

Roger Selner. *Greatest Elk: A Complete Historical and Illustrated Record of North America's Biggest Elk.* Safari Press © 2002.

Dr. Leonard Lee Rue III. *The Encyclopedia of Deer.* Voyageur Press © 2004.

Jack Ballard. *Falcon Pocket Guide Moose.* Falcon Guides © 2014.

Marco Festa-Bianchet and Steve D. Côté. *Mountain Goats: Ecology, Behavior, and Conservation of an Alpine Ungulate.* Island Press © 2007.

Douglas H. Chadwick. *A Beast the Color of Winter: The Mountain Goat Observed.* Bison Books © 2002.

INTERNET RESOURCES

National Geographic—Elk
https://www.nationalgeographic.com/animals/mammals/e/elk/

Washington Department of Wildlife—Living with Wildlife: Deer
http://wdfw.wa.gov/living/deer.html

Mooseworld
http://www.mooseworld.com/

American Expedition—Moose Information, Photos & Facts
https://americanexpedition.us/learn-about-wildlife/moose-facts-information-and-photos/

Rocky Mountain Goat Alliance
https://goatalliance.org/

EDUCATIONAL VIDEOS

Access these videos with your smartphone or use the URLs below to find them online.

Elk stags go to town as they battle for the right to mate.

http://x-qr.net/1DR3

Industrial development undermines winter grazing grounds for pronghorn near Yellowstone National Park.

http://x-qr.net/1DNL

Watch as a mother moose protects her new baby from a pack of wolves.

http://x-qr.net/1HDb

Nimble-footed mountain goats scale cliffs with over sixty-degree inclines!

http://x-qr.net/1Hap

Some of the world's most incredible migrations of deer take place in the Greater Yellowstone ecosystem.

http://x-qr.net/1ENf